COLORADO AVALANCHE

BY WILL GRAVES

Copyright © 2023 by Press Room Editions. All rights reserved. No part of this book may be used or reproduced in any manner whatsoever, including internet usage, without written permission from the copyright owner, except in the case of brief quotations embodied in critical articles and reviews.

Book design by Maggie Villaume
Cover design by Maggie Villaume

Photographs ©: David Zalubowski/AP Images, cover; Andrew Bershaw/Icon Sportswire, 4–5, 9, 29; Phelan Ebenhack/AP Images, 7; Dave Tenenbaum/AP Images, 10–11; Kevin Larkin/AP Images, 13; Paul Chiasson/Canadian Press/AP Images, 15; Bill Janscha/AP Images, 16–17; Ryan Remiorz/Canadian Press/AP Images, 19; Icon Sports Media/Icon Sportswire, 21; Dustin Bradford/Icon Sportswire, 23; Tony Gutierrez/AP Images, 24–25; Scott D. Stivason/Cal Sport Media/AP Images, 26

Press Box Books, an imprint of Press Room Editions.

ISBN
978-1-63494-592-9 (library bound)
978-1-63494-610-0 (paperback)
978-1-63494-645-2 (epub)
978-1-63494-628-5 (hosted ebook)

Library of Congress Control Number: 2022913236

Distributed by North Star Editions, Inc.
2297 Waters Drive
Mendota Heights, MN 55120
www.northstareditions.com

Printed in the United States of America
Mankato, MN
012023

ABOUT THE AUTHOR
Will Graves has worked for more than two decades as a sports journalist and since 2011 has served as correspondent for The Associated Press in Pittsburgh, Pennsylvania, where he covers the NHL, the NFL, and Major League Baseball as well as various Olympic sports.

TABLE OF CONTENTS

CHAPTER 1
BEST TEAM WINS
5

CHAPTER 2
WOE CANADA
11

CHAPTER 3
AT THIER PEAK
17

SUPERSTAR PROFILE
NATHAN MACKINNON
22

CHAPTER 4
DYNAMITE IN DENVER
25

QUICK STATS 30
GLOSSARY 31
TO LEARN MORE 32
INDEX 32

1

Nathan MacKinnon lines up a shot in the 2022 Stanley Cup Final.

BEST TEAM WINS

Expectations were high in Colorado for the 2022 playoffs. The Avalanche came in with the best record in the Western Conference. Boasting a deep and talented roster, the Avs looked ready for a deep playoff run. Now it was time to prove it.

The Avs lost just two games in their first three playoff series. Then they jumped out to a 3–1 series lead in the Stanley Cup Final.

One more win would secure the National Hockey League (NHL) championship. But no win is easy in the Final. And no team knew how to win like the two-time defending champion Tampa Bay Lightning.

Facing elimination, the Lightning won Game 5 in Colorado. Then center Steven Stamkos put the Lightning up 1–0 early in Game 6. The Tampa crowd was buzzing. That's when one of the Avalanche's biggest stars stepped up.

Nathan MacKinnon got off to a fast start in the second period. After having a shot saved, he positioned himself in the left face-off circle. Teammate Bowen Byram had the puck near the blue line. MacKinnon raised his stick in the air

Artturi Lehkonen scored eight goals in the 2022 playoffs.

to show he was open. When the pass arrived, MacKinnon blasted a one-timer. The puck screamed past the Tampa Bay goalie to tie the game 1–1. That was MacKinnon's 13th goal of the playoffs. No player had scored more.

A little over 10 minutes later, the Avalanche sprung a three-on-two break. MacKinnon, in the center, passed the puck to his right. A Tampa defenseman tapped it. But the puck still found the stick of left winger Artturi Lehkonen. He fired a snap shot into the back of the net. It counted as an assist for MacKinnon. And it proved to be the game-winning goal.

AVALANCHE FOR THE AGES

Since 1987, a team must win 16 playoff games in order to lift the Stanley Cup. That means winning four best-of-seven series. The Avs finished their 2022 Cup run 16–4. Only the 1988 Oilers had fewer losses before winning the Cup.

The Avalanche tied an NHL record with 10 comeback victories during the 2022 playoffs.

The Avalanche won the Stanley Cup for the first time in 21 years. With some of the league's brightest young stars in the game, the Avs looked like they would contend for years to come.

2

Mario Gosselin played his first six seasons in Quebec.

WOE CANADA

The Colorado Avalanche didn't begin in Colorado. They didn't even begin in the NHL. The team started in 1972 as the Quebec Nordiques. They played in a league called the World Hockey Association (WHA).

The WHA tried to compete with the NHL. But the upstart league folded in 1979. Not all of the teams stopped playing, though. Four WHA teams made the jump to the NHL. The Nordiques were one of them. However, Quebec had a hard time winning in a new league.

The Nordiques of the 1980s had stars. Forward Michel Goulet was a regular All-Star. Brothers Peter, Anton, and Marian Stastny all played on the same line for the Nordiques. Peter was the best of the bunch. He piled up 1,048 points in 10 seasons. But all those goals did not lead to team success.

Teenage phenom Joe Sakic arrived in 1988. The star center scored with ease right away. But the Nordiques still didn't win much.

By the mid-1990s, a change was needed. In 1995, the team moved

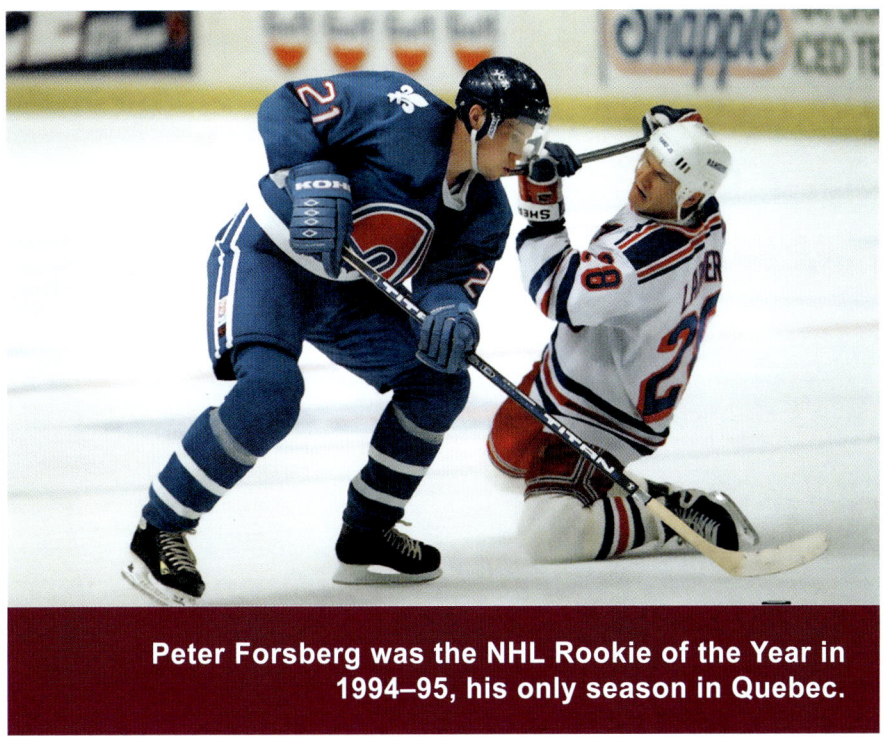

Peter Forsberg was the NHL Rookie of the Year in 1994–95, his only season in Quebec.

to Denver. The Colorado Avalanche were born.

The new city brought quick success. Sakic made the move. The Avalanche had another young star in center Peter Forsberg. What they needed was a goalie. They found one in Patrick Roy.

He had won two Stanley Cups with the Montreal Canadiens. Colorado traded for him in December 1995. Roy wasted little time making an impact. The Avalanche went all the way to the Stanley Cup Final. In 16 seasons in Quebec, the team had never made it that far.

Roy saved his best performance for last. The Avs won the first three games against the Florida Panthers. Roy turned aside all 63 shots he faced in Game 4. The game still went to triple overtime.

•SECOND CHANCE

The Avalanche weren't the first NHL team to play in Denver. The Kansas City Scouts moved to the Mile High City in 1976. They were renamed the Colorado Rockies. The fun didn't last long. The Rockies were sold in 1982. They moved to New Jersey and became the Devils.

Patrick Roy makes a save against the Florida Panthers in the 1996 Stanley Cup Final.

Finally a Uwe Krupp slapshot gave the Avalanche a four-game sweep. Colorado fans saw the Cup raised in the team's first year in town.

3

Joe Sakic won the Hart Trophy, which is awarded to the league's Most Valuable Player (MVP), in 2000–01.

AT THEIR PEAK

The Avalanche got off to a hot start in Denver. They barely cooled off over the next decade.

Having a gifted playmaker like Joe Sakic certainly helped. Sakic wasn't among the biggest players around. But he made up for his 5-foot-11 (180 cm) frame by outworking opponents. He spent countless hours practicing his shot. That helped him score a team record 625 goals over 20 seasons.

The team believed in Sakic so much it named him captain at age 23. He kept that title for 16 seasons.

Sakic hardly did it alone. Powerful forward Peter Forsberg added some scoring punch. Patrick Roy was one of the sport's all-time great goalies. The Avs looked like they had the talent to win more Stanley Cups. But the Detroit Red Wings kept getting in the way. The two teams became fierce rivals in the late 1990s. They regularly clashed on the ice. During one game in 1997, nine different fights broke out.

Colorado finally returned to the Stanley Cup Final in 2001. Ray Bourque was a big reason why. The defenseman

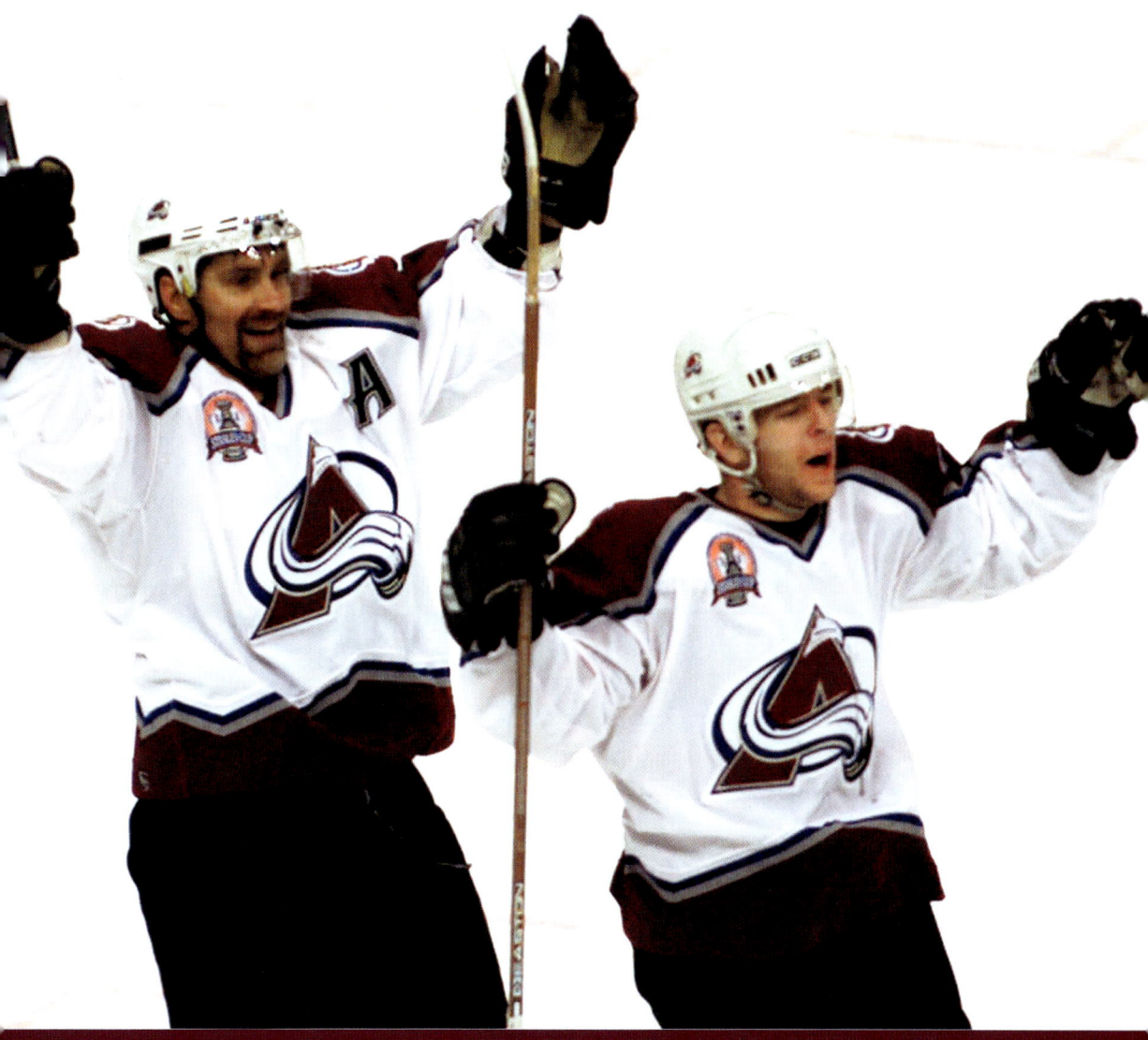

Ray Bourque (left) and Alex Tanguay celebrate a teammate's goal in the 2001 Stanley Cup Final.

spent his first 20 seasons with the Boston Bruins. He won five Norris Trophies there. That award is given to the NHL's best defenseman each season. But he never won a Stanley Cup.

The Bruins wanted to give him one last shot. So they traded him to Colorado. The Avs faced the New Jersey Devils in the Final. The series went a full seven games. Sakic's second-period goal in Game 7 helped secure a 3–1 victory.

Lifting the Stanley Cup is hockey's biggest honor. And tradition says the team captain lifts it first. Not in 2001. Sakic handed the famous trophy to

AVALANCHE OF SUCCESS

The team won two division titles in 16 years in Quebec. Once it moved to Colorado, it won nine straight division titles between 1995 and 2003. That was the longest streak in NHL history.

Ray Bourque lifts the Stanley Cup in 2001.

Bourque first. Tears streamed down Bourque's face as he kissed the Cup.

• SUPERSTAR PROFILE

NATHAN MACKINNON

Nathan MacKinnon grew up in Cole Harbour, Nova Scotia. That's also where fellow Canadian star Sidney Crosby grew up. Like Crosby, MacKinnon was a teenager when he was taken with the first pick in the NHL Draft.

It did not take long for MacKinnon to become a star. He used his blinding speed to take the league by storm. The center won the Calder Memorial Trophy in 2014. That's given to the league's top rookie. Three times in his first nine seasons MacKinnon was a finalist for the Hart Memorial Trophy.

When he was 14, MacKinnon saw Crosby bring the Stanley Cup to Cole Harbour. MacKinnon dreamed of doing the same one day. At 26, MacKinnon hoisted the Cup with the Avalanche. He brought it home to Cole Harbour later that summer.

Through the 2021–22 season, Nathan MacKinnon tallied 648 points in 638 games.

4

Gabriel Landeskog won the Calder Memorial Trophy in 2011–12.

DYNAMITE IN DENVER

The Avalanche thought highly of Gabriel Landeskog. They proved that by naming the steady forward their captain before the 2012–13 season. At 19 he was the youngest captain in NHL history. The rebuilding was only just beginning. Colorado had the first pick in the 2013 draft. It selected Nathan MacKinnon. The skilled center quickly became the face of the team.

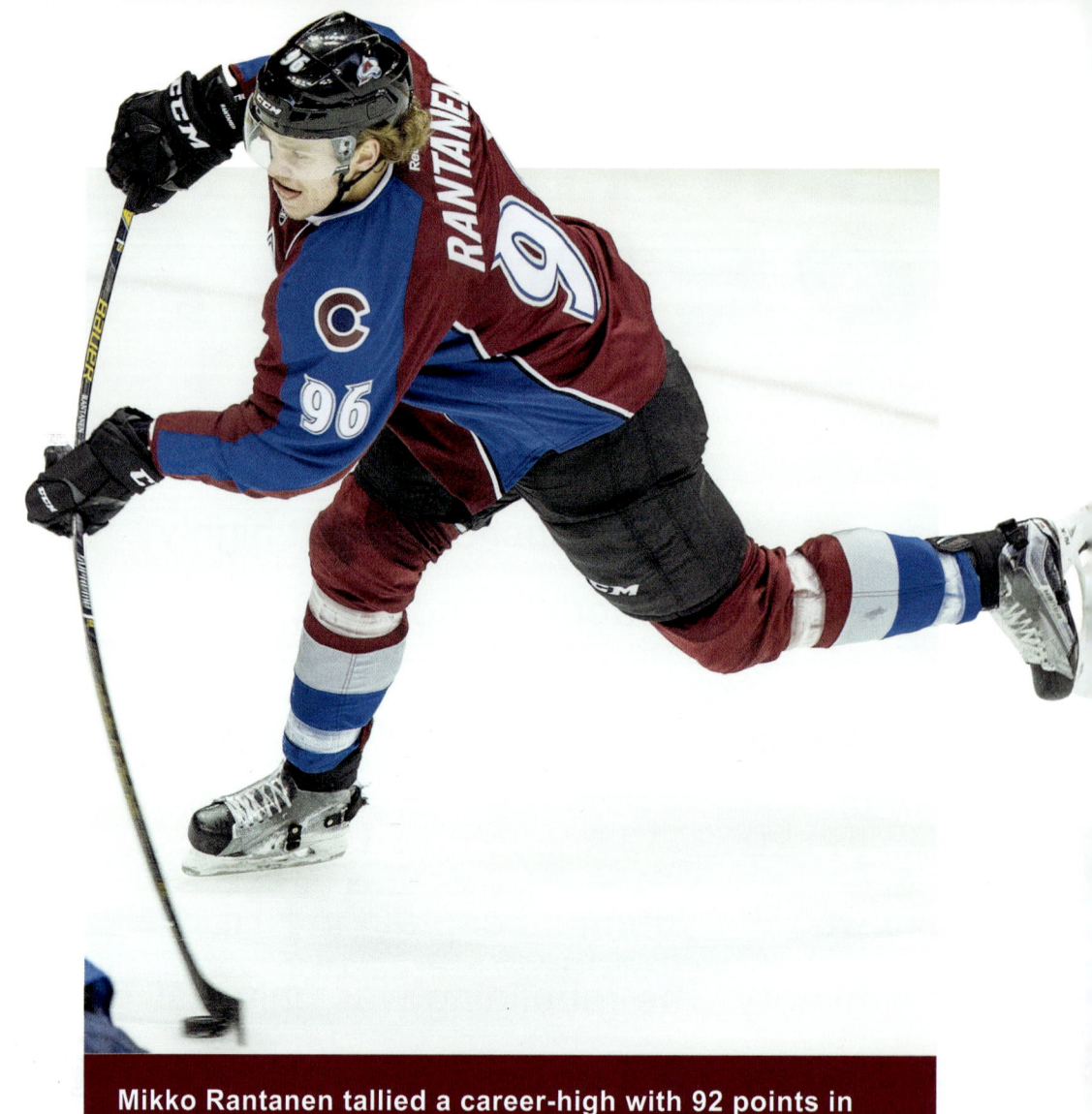

Mikko Rantanen tallied a career-high with 92 points in the 2021–22 season.

The next piece arrived in 2015. Colorado drafted forward Mikko Rantanen. The trio of Landeskog, MacKinnon, and

Rantanen became one of the NHL's best lines. During the 2020–21 season, they combined for 70 goals and 113 assists. Colorado won the Presidents' Trophy after finishing with the best record in the league.

MacKinnon, Rantanen, and Landeskog provided the firepower. Center Nazem Kadri came to the Avalanche to bring an edge. Colorado traded for the fiery Kadri in 2019. He gave a young team a veteran presence. Kadri also improved his game in Colorado. His 87 points in 2021–22 marked a career high.

Cale Makar's arrival during the 2019 playoffs completed the rebuilding process. Makar is the rare defenseman who has elite offensive skills. He set a team record for points by a defenseman in 2021–22 with 86. That helped him win the Norris Trophy.

Colorado could overpower its opponents. Makar was a big reason why. The Avs started their 2022 playoff run with a sweep of the Nashville Predators. Makar dominated in the series. He became the first defenseman in NHL history to record 10 points in a four-game series. Makar went on to record 29 points in the playoffs. That was good enough to earn

A DAZZLING DEBUT

Cale Makar made his NHL debut in the 2019 playoffs. The Avs were playing the Calgary Flames. Makar ended up scoring a goal on his first shot in the NHL. He was the first defenseman to score while making his debut in the playoffs.

Cale Makar won the Conn Smythe Trophy, which is awarded to the MVP of the playoffs, in 2022.

him the Conn Smythe Trophy as the Avs won their third Stanley Cup. With Makar and MacKinnon leading the way, Avs fans hoped a dynasty was in the making.

COLORADO AVALANCHE
QUICK STATS

TEAM HISTORY: Quebec Nordiques (1972–95), Colorado Avalanche (1995–)

STANLEY CUP CHAMPIONSHIPS: 3 (1996, 2001, 2022)

KEY COACHES:

- Marc Crawford (1994–98), 135 wins, 75 losses, 36 ties
- Bob Hartley (1998–2002), 193 wins, 108 losses, 48 ties, 10 overtime losses
- Jared Bednar (2016–), 240 wins, 168 losses, 46 overtime losses

HOME ARENA: Ball Arena (Denver, CO)

MOST CAREER POINTS: Joe Sakic (1,641)

MOST CAREER GOALS: Joe Sakic (625)

MOST CAREER ASSISTS: Joe Sakic (1,016)

MOST CAREER SHUTOUTS: Patrick Roy (37)

*Stats are accurate through the 2021–22 season

GLOSSARY

CAPTAIN
A team's leader.

DRAFT
An event that allows teams to choose new players coming into a league.

ELITE
The best of the best.

OVERTIME
An additional period of play to decide a game's winner.

PHENOM
A person who is extremely talented at a young age.

RIVAL
An opposing player or team that brings out the greatest emotion from fans and players.

ROOKIE
A professional athlete in his or her first year of competition.

VETERAN
A player who has spent several years in a league.

TO LEARN MORE

BOOKS

Davidson, B. Keith. *NHL*. New York: Crabtree Publishing, 2022.

Duling, Kaitlyn. *Women in Hockey*. Lake Elmo, MN: Focus Readers, 2020.

Price, Karen. *Nathan MacKinnon: Hockey Superstar*. Mendota Heights, MN: North Star Editions, 2019.

MORE INFORMATION

To learn more about the Colorado Avalanche, go to **pressboxbooks.com/AllAccess**.

These links are routinely monitored and updated to provide the most current information available.

INDEX

Bourque, Ray, 18, 21
Byram, Bowen, 6
Crosby, Sidney, 22
Forsberg, Peter, 13, 18
Goulet, Michel, 12

Kadri, Nazem, 27
Krupp, Uwe, 15
Landeskog, Gabriel, 25–27
Lehkonen, Artturi, 8
MacKinnon, Nathan, 6–8, 22, 25–27, 29
Makar, Cale, 27–29

Rantanen, Mikko, 26–27
Roy, Patrick, 13–14, 18
Sakic, Joe, 12–13, 17–18, 20
Stastny, Anton, 12
Stastny, Marian, 12
Stastny, Peter, 12